Prairie Town

Story and Illustrations by
Ryan Durney

This is prairie town.
Prairie dogs live in this town.

Prairie dogs climb out of their burrows.

They kiss with their noses to say hello.

Prairie dogs eat grass, roots, seeds and green plants.

Prairie dogs build burrows. They use their paws to dig.

They use their noses to pat the dirt.

Prairie dogs work, but they love to play too!